Trombones:

A Sonnet Crown

and other poems

a remix of
James Weldon Johnson's
God's Trombones
in sonnet form

Raymond D. Maxwell

DEDICATION

This collection is dedicated to the memory of my father, Raymond R. Maxwell (1913-1980), who loved poetry, and my grandfather, Walter J. Maxwell (1883-1954), who wrote church songs.

ACKNOWLEDGEMENTS

The Aaron Douglas illustrations in James Weldon Johnson's God's Trombones: Seven Negro Sermons in Verse provided the inspiration for this attempt at a sonnet crown. Each sonnet is in turn based on each one of the Johnson sermons, borrows its title, and ends with an actual line from the sermon it represents.

The original Johnson text and the Douglas illustrations are available here: http://docsouth.unc.edu/southlit/johnson/johnson.html

CONTENTS

Trombones – a sonnet crown

INTRODUCTION

NaPoWriMo, National Poetry Writing Month, is a month (April) when poetry devotees commit to writing at least one poem per day. In 2016, I ignored most of the NaPoWriMo prompts and drew inspiration from things, events, happenings in my daily life.

Early in the month I attended three events that had a huge impact on my April writing. The first one was a writing salon at a local art gallery, a short, three hour "class," that looked at one piece of art from various perspectives and encouraged attendees to write about the experience. The second was a poetry reading at a local library by three poets, sonnet writers, who read from their works and spoke about the "sonnet" craft. The third was a lunch time exhibition talk about a single piece of art.

I decided to try my hand at a "crown of sonnets," also called a "corona." All the sonnet writers I saw at the reading talked about it! I would base each sonnet on a unique piece of art, implementing the tools we used in the writing salon. Finally, I'd use as the art work a series of paintings used as illustrations for poetry, and the exhibition talk I attended provided such an example, one in a series of paintings by the famed Harlem Renaissance painter, Aaron Douglas, used to illustrate James Weldon Johnson's "God's Trombones, Seven Negro Sermons in Verse," which was on exhibit.

The original Johnson text and the Douglas illustrations are available here: http://docsouth.unc.edu/southlit/johnson/johnson.html

Methodology: In a sonnet crown, the final line of each poem becomes the first line of each succeeding poem, and the first line of the first poem, the final line of the last poem. I tried as closely as possible to make each final line align with a line from the original Johnson poetry, God's Trombones, that the Aaron Douglas art work illustrated. Finally, because the example I saw on exhibit was the illustration for the final sermon in the series, The Judgment Day, I worked my way through the original sermons from back to front, giving the whole thing a slightly different twist. I encourage the reader to seek out the original Douglas illustrations, online, in the hardbound version of the Johnson collection, or, if you are lucky, the originals in exhibition.

After the sonnet crown, I include some poems I am reading at the 2016 Caswell and Emily Maxwell Family Reunion in Burlington, NC. I end with some NaPoWriMo poems from previous years.

More of my poems are available here: https://thisismypoetryblog.wordpress.com/

Thank you for reading and enjoy!

Trombones – a sonnet crown

THE SONNET CROWN

Raymond D. Maxwell

The Judgment Day

It's more than just a painting or a poem –
or even a sonnet for a painting
(we'd be so vain to suggest!). The story
is far greater than the sum of its parts.

The judgment day is what we seek, and fear.
In no hurry to pay for our misdeeds,
give us reparations now for insults,
moral crimes against us, past and present.

There is a discrimination – between
the sinner and the saved, darkness dwellers,
those who see the light. Salvation's shining
ray uplifts the soul; lightning bolts reveal
the lumps of lead the wicked thought were pots
of earthly gold. And time shall be no more.

Let My People Go

Of earthly gold. And time shall be no more.
I ride the steed of war, my spear sharpened
to kill my brother at Pharaoh's command.
But there's a light that pierces all the waves,
the rage of hate, and separates our thoughts
from the darkened state of eternal war.

Go up, Moses, tell old Pharaoh to go.
We no longer need his tricks and trinkets,
his crutches enabled our servitude.
Tell Pharaoh he needs us - we don't need him.
Without us, he, his army cease to be.
Give old Pharaoh the 4-1-1. We're done.
No more blues, no more weeping over me.
The groans of my people have filled my ears.

The Crucifixion

The groans of my people have filled my ears.
A line of folks awaits the lynching tree
behind our dear, sweet Jesus. Simon bears
the cross for him, climbs up the rugged road.
Sweet Jesus. Nails go through his hands, his feet –
the soldier's spear pierces him. Mary weeps,
we weep when we think about how he died.

I tremble. My turn's next. The rope is loose
around my neck. The crowd screams, "Crucify!"
We bear the cross. We die on Calvary.
The soldiers stare, do nothing. The thorny crown,
the purple robe mock. Sweet Jesus. Betrayed.
The traitor's bitter kiss, its passion lost –
the sweat like drops of blood upon his brow.

Noah Built the Ark

The sweat like drops of blood upon his brow.
"He is working so hard to build that boat,
He's gonna give himself a heart attack!"
His wife would say. Year after passing year
he worked on the Ark, rain or shine, hot, cold,
through periods of ridicule, self doubt -
building, preaching.
                              Legend says he gathered
two of every living creature before
he sealed the hatch. Then the raining began.
Forty days. The rising waters lifted
the Ark off its blocks - sent it underway.
For one year they sailed. Sea without a shore.
Then God gave Noah a sign - a Rainbow -
it won't be water, but fire - next time.

Go Down Death – A Funeral Sermon

It won't be water, but fire – next time.
The universe was expanding faster
than we thought, the distance the death angel
had to travel, longer, his flight angle
trajectory, steeper than allowed for
in previous calculations. A bright
star steered him to the house of Caroline,
our sister, to commence her journey home.

Death didn't say a word. She saw Death come
like a falling star, our Caroline. No fear
was in her heart. Death took her in his arms
like a baby, comforted her, placed her
on his horse securely for the ride.
And she whispered to us: I'm going home.

The Prodigal Son

And she whispered to us: I'm going home.
The young man traveled down the easy road
to Babylon. New clothes, new dancing friends,
new drinking dens and gambling games to play,
and women – flowery scents intoxicate
the mind. Oh the women of Babylon!

But his luck ran out – good times disappeared
and he found himself stripped of everything
good fortune gave him. Soon he cast his lot
among the beasts, the scavengers, the swine
who thrived on leftovers, things tossed aside –
with beggars in the mire of Babylon.
Then, in disgust, he made the journey home.
Young man — your arms too short to box with God.

The Creation

Young man - your arms too short to box with God.
Invisible hand traversed time's flow
and made a world to cure his loneliness.
A thousand worlds. But that was not enough.
There was a need to correspond, to speak,
to apprehend what thoughts the space contained
his hands had wrought. So God created man.

From dust and clay he shaped the human form,
then breathed into his mouth the breath of life.
And man became what God intended him
to be, a maker of his own image.
Then plants grew near him, symbiotically,
providing food and warmth - to each - in turn.
And man became a living soul. Amen.

Listen Lord - A Prayer

And man became a living soul. Amen.
We lift our prayers, our noble thoughts to Thee,
our source of strength and creativity.
These words, these phrases - our meditation,
we presently petition at your throne.
But listen, Lord, just between you and me,
things ain't so right down here. The folks you left
in charge have gone astray - the golden calf
is all they seek, an idol that they made
with their own hands. Keep us in your light, Lord,
on the righteous path. Forgive the sinners,
languishing in Babylon. Take pity
on the poets and artists who fall short.
It's more than just a painting or a poem.

FAMILY REUNION POEMS

Raymond D. Maxwell

In Memoriam: Grandpap Dick Rankin

First of all, thank you for visiting the cemetery
every now and then, and cleaning the graves

of the old folks. New generations have forgotten,
but they wouldn't be, now, if we had not been then.

When I was barely a boy, I run off with the rebel
soldiers,
did odd jobs, cooked for them, tended to the
horses.

None of us farmers knew that much about war.
Legend is true, I returned to Browns Summit with a
box full

of Confederate money. Warn't no count, no way.
Rebel soldiers give it to me. I swear. It was my
pay.

Buried that box in a tobacco field in Jackson after
the war,
same field where I buried mason jars of moonshine
I made,

to keep it cool and to hide it from the revenuers.
Cool on a summer day. Best in Guilford County,

the white folks used to say. The war freed the slaves, or
so they said. I didn't know much about politics, still don't,

or taking sides, or fighting, but I did know we had a good master,
a kind, Christian man. Now your daddy and his sister were just children

when I transferred to the next world. But I watched them grow up and
tried to take care of them, best I could. It ain't easy

moving back and forth between worlds. And yes, I made
a bit of moonshine in my day. Drank a little, too,

more towards the end. Best in Guilford County. Hid it from the revenuers. Cool on a hot summer day.

Prayer Song to Grandma Lena Rankin Maxwell

Early, early in the morning
just before the break of day,
I arise, and count my blessings,
and fall to my knees to pray.
And I thank the Gracious Master
and I praise His name so sweet,
and I pour out all my troubles,
and I leave them at His feet.

"Prayer is better," said the wise man
"than another hour's snooze,
it will lift you up much higher
than some other stuff you use."

Late at evening after dealing
With the problems of the day,
All bewildered and disheartened
I fall to my knees and pray.
And I thank the Gracious Master
for his grace in helping me
through another day of passage
on life's cold and stormy sea.

"Prayer is better," said the wise man
"than that wine or weed or dope.
It will soothe away your heartache,
it will fill you up with hope."

Going fishing with Daddy

Going fishing with Daddy
in Browns Summit
was about as good as good got:
Saturday at sunset,
electrical jobs all done and
poetry memorized.
Time for some fun!

Long cane pole,
worms from the spring bed,
fish too small to eat –
but catching 'em was fun anyway.

Daddy's long gone,
and the fishing pond is dead too –
irrigation for some organic tobacco fields –
what's left is a smaller,
dark brown puddle,
and poison ivy,
and chiggars on wild blackberries
where the edge used to be.

Epistle #7

Thank you for the fishing trips,
and the science fair helps,

each time you took me
with you to work,
and each piece of advice
that fell from your trembling lips -
wouldn't be the same without
your presence, good or ill.

Some buds on the rose bushes

Some buds on the rose bushes
are barely visible, tiny, hidden
between thorns and leaves.
Some, fully blossomed, attract
our vision, their fragrance, our
noses and our wandering thoughts.

The buds between appeal only
to the bees and butterflies,
and to careful gardeners with
pruning shears. My mother wore
white gloves when she "cut up"
the rose bushes, and a wide-brimmed hat,
and a scarf wrapped round her neck.

Summa Cum Laude

"She delights the earth with her footsteps,
and in speaking, fulfills the desires of the deaf"

A flower, a synesthetic glow...
An inflorescent melody
(in search of combination)
That violates its meter
And disregards its rhythm
(as defined by classic standards)
To uphold its right to grow.

A pearl, a diamond, cast among swine...
Tomorrow is retrieved from the rubbish
And polished to a more brilliant luster.

A vessel, undefiled,
Well-built and well-prepared:
To weather all the storms and blasts;
To sail the oceans, deep and vast;
To overcome the dark morass;
To persevere until the last –
And with me, heaven, share.

End of Life Criteria

like a piano tune
that starts and ends,
so is life ...

death cuts in:
a toneless key;
a nameless chord;
a sharp discontinuity ...

judgment occurs
without a moment's notice;
and on the second half
one regrets not doing
what should have been done ...

every second is judgment -
and every opportunity
affords one yet another
to correct the incorrection -
before the final hour ...
has passed.

Thoughts about judgment day

the hour actively approaches
while we, its victims, sit and wait,
with folded arms,
trying to appear comfortable
and carefree,
and mutually exclusive.

Days pass quickly, and nights,
like the blink of an eye....
nay, the pupil's dilation.
Time races to its destination
while we, in our lethargy,
approximate suspended animation.

There are no conclusions,
only the vain pleadings
for another sequel,
a few more hours,
a couple more opportunities.

The rope by which we hang is long,
but the knot is sure.

SELECTED NaPoWriMo POEMS

Raymond D. Maxwell

Ottava Rima (2013)

I do not have a poem to say today,
Appalling how thoughts sometimes hit a wall:
The words don't seem to flow, a sad cliché
That accurately spells with great recall
My present state where words have gone astray,
Imagination covered by a pall.
But just as long as ink is in my pen,
I'll find my Muse and write a poem again.

A triolet (2013)

> Sem ti, tudo me enoja e me aborrece
> sem ti, perpetuamente estou passando,
> nas mores alegrias, mor tristeza. - Camoes

I'm not long for this world of woe -
of strife and quarrelsome divide;
so I'll content myself with poems -
I'm not long for this world of woe.
In time we reap the deeds we sow:
Our words and acts and thoughts collide –
I'm not long for this world of woe –
of strife and quarrelsome divide.

April 28, 2013

The words we read,
the lines we write are gaps
in time, that soon take flight –

poetry has that property
transporting us through space –
we write a word and make a rhyme
and aim it to its place –

if accurate, we hit the mark,
we reach the goal we seek –
but if precise, we claim the prize,
and scale the highest peak –

the words and rhymes unwind, divide
with measured purpose, need –
then seek to replicate the thought
and shape the world of deeds –

The message in the poems we write
is free, yet hidden in plain sight.

Bernini's Apollo and Daphne (2014)

Daphne is fleeing Apollo
and her face is an open book of terror.
She'd rather be a laurel tree
than live the captive life
of an object of once passionate pursuit.
Apollo's hand slips around her waist,
her abdomen already transforming to bark,
yet through the wood he feels in her gut
her beating, throbbing heart,
and he, his passion a misdirected vector,
could not care less. Look at his face.
His focus is the hunt, the game,
her fingers leaves, her arms now laurel branches.
The transformation is a meditation.

Reminiscences on my parents' 61st anniversary

We eat Chinese food on Fridays, mostly,
fish makes it sort of Catholic, partly,
and having it on Fridays is Islamic
and Jewish, maybe. Truth is we are not
religious at all. We have made peace
with our choices and our burial preferences
are listed in our wills. I do regret
my youthful indiscretions, the time I snuck
off my boat on a duty day, the night
I spent with a girl who turned out to be
a drug dealer could have been my last,
not for drugs, mind you, let's be clear.
A cute, sweet girl, a Georgia peach,
a country girl my mother would have loved.

Remembering Prince

Let's be clear.
The winners want this world
to be the only one.
They don't need a heaven,
a nirvana, a promised land,
a garden with black-eyed virgins
after martyrdom.

The winners want this world
to last forever and a day,
no disruption, no inherent degradation
in the plan/to the plan that keeps them
in charge, the religion that justifies,
the philosophy that rationalizes,
the mathematics that computes
their equations.

Let's be clear, again.
At length, soon or late,
things unravel. Entropy rules,
permanence becomes impermanent,
time folds back on itself,
like Prince says, his music
for the future written in the past
and stored in a vault – a chess game
that anybody can learn to play and win.

Once upon a time (a backwards fairytale)

And everybody lived happily ever after –
after the plants started sprouting again,
after the birds started singing again,
after all the poisoned debris was cleared
& destroyed buildings were repurposed –
after the hospital overcrowding was relieved
and the population cured of radioactive exposure –
after the clouded skies were cleared of floating ash
& the rivers & streams, of chemical wastes –
after pandemonium & chaos ruled the streets –
after stores & shops were looted for food
& supplies, & drinking water – after the politicians
made the decisions & dropped the atom bombs as
they promised in their campaigns –
once upon a time.

April 29, 2016

I never made it up to Aleppo.
There was property there to inspect,
a perfect reason to take a day off
and drive up, get away from all
the random sameness of Damascus.
But we kept putting it off.

the first time I listened to Zooid
I could hear traces of Arkestra
wafting through – the juxtaposition
of high-pitched and low tones,
the improvised piano keeping the rhythm,
the pizzicato of the bass strings
gave it all away.

But we kept putting it off. Then,
we transferred back, still assuming
we'd return at some point and trek
up to Aleppo to see the remains
of an ancient civilization.

so when Threadgill said Sun Ra
was one of his important influences
it only confirmed my suspicions.
The remains of a former civilization.
Now it might be too late.

Trombones – a sonnet crown

Raymond D. Maxwell

ABOUT THE AUTHOR

Ray Maxwell is from Greensboro, NC. He started writing poetry in elementary school. He joined the Navy in 1978 and served aboard two submarines, the USS Hammerhead, SSN-663, and the USS Michigan, SSBN 727 (B). At the end of his enlistment he attended Florida A&M University, where he graduated summa cum laude, received a Naval Commission, and was assigned to the USS Luce, DDG-38.

Upon completion of naval service, Ray joined the Foreign Service, with assignments in countries in West Africa (Guinea-Bissau, Angola, and Ghana), the UK, the Middle East (Egypt, Iraq, and Syria) and Washington. He has graduate degrees from the School of Oriental and African Studies (University of London) and the Catholic University of America.

Ray lives in Washington, DC with his wife, Filomena.

Made in the USA
Middletown, DE
12 April 2022